TRUE MUMMY

True Mummy

(a play)

TOM CONE

Anvil Press Publishers | 2004
Vancouver | Canada

True Mummy
Copyright © 2004 by Tom Cone

NATIONAL LIBRARY OF CANADA CATALOGUING IN PUBLICATION DATA

Cone, Tom, 1948-
  True Mummy / Tom Cone.

(Anvil Performance Series, ISSN: 1188-0872; no. 5)

  A play.
  ISBN 1-895636-52-3

  I. Title.
PS8555.O52T78 2003   C812'.54   C2003-911022-2

Printed and bound in Canada
Cover by Typesmith Design
Typesetting by HeimatHouse

Represented in Canada by the Literary Press Group
Distributed by the University of Toronto Press

All inquiries regarding production rights should be addressed to The Joyce Ketay Agency, 630 Ninth Avenue, Suite 706, New York, NY 10036.

The publisher gratefully acknowledges the financial assistance of the B.C. Arts Council, the Canada Council for the Arts, and the Book Publishing Industry Development Program (BPIDP) for their support of our publishing program.

Anvil Press
P.O. Box 3008, Main Post Office
Vancouver, B.C. V6B 3X5
CANADA
www.anvilpress.com

For Myros Buriak

I would like to thank Karen Matthews,
and our daughter, Ruby Cone

I would also like to acknowledge:
The staff of The Playwrights Theatre Centre
Northern Lights Theatre
Linda Hoffman

Characters:
PATTI: a sculptor, early 30s
CAROLINE: a fire-spotter, middle 40s to 50
STANLEY: a rabbi who sells life insurance, 50 years of age
EGYPTIAN PRINCESS: 12-13 years of age

True Mummy was first produced in a tri-production
arrangement between the Playwrights Theatre Centre in
Vancouver, The Vancouver East Cultural Centre, and The
Vancouver Playhouse Theatre Company. The premiere
production was presented at the Vancouver East Cultural
Centre from February 24 to March 16, 1996 with the
following cast:

> Patti: . . . . Lorretta Bailey
> Caroline: . . . . Susan Hogan
> Stanley: . . . . Alec Willows

Directed by Kim Selody. Set Design by Joost Bakker.
Costume Design by Karen Matthews. Original soundscape
by Peter Hannan.

A significantly revised version of *True Mummy* was produced
by Northern Lights Theatre from March 26 to April 6, 1997
with the following cast:

> Egyptian Princess: . . . . Jessica Carmichael
> Patti: . . . . Stephanie Wolfe
> Caroline: . . . . Jill Dyck
> Stanley: . . . . Brian Taylor

Directed by DD Kugler. Set Design by Melinda Sutton.
Costume Design by Dean'na Finnman. Slide guitar composition written and performed by Ellen McIlwaine.

FOREWORD

I first came across *True Mummy* in a *Globe and Mail* review
by Chris Dafoe of the Playwrights Theatre Centre (PTC)
premiere production at the Vancouver East Cultural Centre.
Dafoe described a "dreamlike reality . . . discussions on love,
death, morality and art . . . casual, and not-so-casual
exploitations of one another." I was intrigued. I phoned
PTC Artistic Director Kim Selody, he sent the 120-page
script, and I brazenly phoned Tom Cone—a senior play-
wright whom I'd never met.

Tom?

Yes?

I'm Artistic Director of Northern Light Theatre in
Edmonton, and I just read the draft of *True Mummy* that
Kim sent me.

Oh, good. Good.

I'm thoroughly engaged by the tensions in the script—
desecration as truthful, immortality in cannibalism, death as
transformation. I especially like how your characters wrestle
with, and embody, these ideas.

That's great. Thanks.

But I think it's overwritten.

OK.

A lot.

Uh-huh.

By a factor of two. Maybe more.

[Silence.]

Tom?

Yes?

I could be wrong.

I invited Tom to use an upcoming Page-to-Stage workshop
at the National Arts Centre as an opportunity to cut all

nuance from the script. I encouraged him to locate the essential, the skeletal, *True Mummy*. If the exercise proved fruitless, I argued, he still had the PTC version. Tom wanted to think about it. A few days later he phoned me, and said:

Let's go for it. I mean if we're going to do this, let's really go for it.

And so we went for it. During four 12-hour days in Ottawa, Tom and I paced the tiny Atelier box office and stripped the often-ornate dialogue to its core. The PTC version of the script alternated realistic scenes with dream sequences. In our most radical move, we cut the dreams even though they were theatrically engaging. We both knew counterpoint scenes were required, and I felt they should, somehow, give 'true mummy' a larger life in the play. I vaguely suggested a series of Egyptology lectures. But writing the counterpoint scenes, whatever they were, would have to come after the workshop. The actors gamely read the script—now less than half its original length—at the public reading (May 30, 1996). It felt a bit flat, but we were exhilarated. The script had arrived at a new beginning.

Shortly after he returned to Vancouver, Tom started faxing me brief scenes that traced the transformation of a young Egyptian girl, from princess, through death, to the surface of Turner's painting. It was an ancient enactment of a re-cycled death—the 'true mummy' counterpoint to the contemporary struggles of Caroline, Stanley, and Patti.

The Northern Light Theatre (NLT) premiere of the radically revised *True Mummy* (March 26 – April 6, 1997) resulted from exceptional individual contributions from every member of the cast and production team. But as you read *True Mummy*, I invite you to imagine the most emblematic elements of our premiere production: the set and light design by Melinda Sutton (with Assistant Narda McCarroll); and the composition and live score by Ellen McIlwaine.

Melinda began with an exhaustive visual research: images of light in empty spaces, the works of Turner, Egyptian mummification procedures, and disturbingly beautiful photos of decaying bodies. We produced the show in Edmonton's former Bus Barns, a space that (at that time) was exactly what you might imagine—cavernous, high-ceilinged, wooden pillars, oil-stained concrete floor. Melinda wanted the natural world of the play represented on stage as an aesthetic artistic construct. In the centre of that deserted industrial wasteland, she began to shape a ritual space, a circle, an island: a huge mound of road crush and fill sand and dirt; ringed on its upstage circumference by six stone (styrofoam) monoliths and fresh-cut willows; upstage-centre a willow sarcophagus; above the sarcophagus, a tall narrow platform upon which the Princess appeared, behind slits of scrim-like material (upon which the final Turner image was projected). Melinda's lighting in the early scenes alternated between the 'natural' locations on the mound, and 'ethereal' Princess above. When the characters entered Patti's studio, however, the harsh side-lighting exposed the artificial construct of the set—and I began to conceive of the entire NLT production as some future work by Patti.

During a visit to Banff, just two weeks after the Ottawa reading of *True Mummy*, I met slide-guitar legend Ellen McIlwaine playing in a local bar. I was knocked out by her relentless drive and consummate technique. When, between sets, she shared the story of her uncompromising artistic life, I was reminded of Patti. I became convinced that Ellen must be part of our production and, shortly after, asked her to compose the score and play it live. She spent a month-long gig in Yellowknife using Middle Eastern chords to compose what she calls 'Egyptian blues.' Upstage, inside the willow sarcophagus, beneath the Princess-platform, McIlwaine played a haunting and raucous slide-guitar score, often accompanied by a keening wail—a musicological link between the death-defying visions of an Egyptian Princess and a fearless contemporary artist.

Enjoy.

—*DD Kugler*
Associate Professor, Theatre Area,
School for the Contemporary Arts,
Simon Fraser University
January, 2004

Act One

SCENE ONE

ON A BEACH

Two people are revealed. PATTI *is lying on her back.* CAROLINE *is giving her mouth to mouth resuscitation. After several frantic attempts* CAROLINE *pulls away.*

— Throat singing

SEGUE TO THE EGYPTIAN PRINCESS

SCENE TWO

The head of a young EGYPTIAN PRINCESS *is revealed. Her head is bound in linen and someone is pulling it tight. We only see the hands of the person binding. The* PRINCESS *winces. Her head continues to be bound while she recites these lines under pain.*

EGYPTIAN PRINCESS

A soft egg
from my chin
to the top
of my head.

A soft egg
like a crown
inside
my skull.

A soft egg
fit
for a princess,
a royal (*winces*)
a royal
shape
like a crown
inside my skull. (*winces, then smiles*)

A soft egg
from my chin
to the top
of my head.

END OF SCENE TWO.

14

SCENE THREE

ON THE BEACH

CAROLINE

(as CAROLINE *pulls away / breathing hard*) Come on
girl! Let's go. (*inhales. mouth to mouth. sits* PATTI
up and bangs her chest) Now! (PATTI *starts to drib-
ble, then cough,* CAROLINE *bangs her back*) You got
it. (PATTI *continues to cough*) Great! How about
one more? Again. Again. You're alive. (*struggle*)
Goddammit you're alive. You beautiful thing.
You're here!

PATTI

(*coming around*) What?

CAROLINE

You're here!

PATTI

(*weak*) What happened?

CAROLINE

Just relax.

PATTI

Tell me!

CAROLINE

You're fine. You're fine.

PATTI

I'm alive?

CAROLINE

You swam out too far.

PATTI

Oh my god! The baby? It's . . .

CAROLINE

You had a baby with you?

PATTI

No, no.

CAROLINE

You're pregnant?

PATTI

Four months.

CAROLINE

Thank God! Hey! They love water, don't they? It's probably wondering why you're so concerned. Here. Lie down now. Knees up. Close your eyes. (*takes* PATTI's *pulse*) Good. We'll just lie here for a minute and then I'll take you up for a hot bath.

PATTI

I drowned?

CAROLINE

I live right up there.

PATTI

(*to herself*) I was floating on my back . . .

CAROLINE

Great view.

PATTI

Trying to photograph myself. . . . Oh my god!
My camera! Shit.

CAROLINE

I didn't see anything.

PATTI

Fuck. No. No.

CAROLINE

I think it's best if you come up and lie down.

PATTI

My camera! Where the hell is it?

CAROLINE

For the baby's sake.

PATTI

I need the camera.

CAROLINE

I'm right up there.

PATTI

I'm serious!

CAROLINE

I know you are. But you've got to think of the
baby.

PATTI

I am thinking of the baby!

CAROLINE

YOU'RE NOT!

PATTI

Fuck you! I'm sorry, I'm sorry. I need my camera.

CAROLINE

I'll take you up and then I'll come back down
and try to find it.

PATTI

I was floating on my back . . . trying to shoot
myself . . . I must have looked dead in the
water. Shit. Do you know how great that is? I
was dead in the water.

CAROLINE

You wanted to look dead?

PATTI

I lost the greatest shot I ever had.

CAROLINE

You were photographing your death?

PATTI

Wouldn't that be incredible? What? You think I
was documenting my suicide? Do I look suici-
dal? I'm having a baby.

CAROLINE

You were dead in the water.

PATTI

It was an accident.

CAROLINE

You took a chance.

PATTI

I had to.

CAROLINE

Let's go.

LIGHTS DOWN.
END OF SCENE THREE.

SCENE FOUR

The EGYPTIAN PRINCESS *is standing still. She is wearing a heavily pleated gown made out of royal linen.*

EGYPTIAN PRINCESS

I'm four steps
to the doors
of a room
I've never been in .
before.
Inside
stand two thousand eyes
waiting for me
to climb those stairs
up to that throne
where I will kneel down
and kiss the feet
of my Queen. My mother. (*pause*)

I'm four steps to the doors.
I cannot wait any longer.

As she takes those steps, we hear the sound of a procession as we segue to the knoll.

END OF SCENE FOUR.

SCENE FIVE

THE KNOLL. NEXT DAY.

PATTI

I was shooting the death of Narcissus. I wanted
bliss. Transcendence. A soothing, deep sleep on
an outgoing tide. I wanted Narcissus travelling
to his death on water. On his back. The colour
of immortal dusk was in the air. A saccharine
smile on his lips. Even in death he's distracted
from what killed him and where he's going.
From the original shots, I would create a death
mask like the one that nearly killed me.
Eventually making a convoy of death masks
bobbing out to sea. A travelling memorial to
distraction. I was trying to make a statement
about the end of our selves. The erosion. The
disappearance. A thousand portraits of Narcissus
going nowhere with that smile. You know that
smile. It's terror gone numb. Frozen. Embalmed
in an avalanche of fear. If fear drives us into
self-absorption, then what follows the death of
Narcissus? The void? Nothingness? The looney
bin.

CAROLINE

Depends on the fear.

PATTI

Cannibalism. Murder.

CAROLINE

Motherhood?

PATTI

Every time I dream of having my baby, I end
up killing and eating him.

21

CAROLINE

What do you mean?

PATTI

I kill the future I need so badly. It's bizarre. Like
last night I dreamt that you and I were hunting
and shooting, and we heard a scream and ran up
and saw an arrow stuck into the ground like a
punctured tummy. I pulled the arrow out and
the ground screamed again. It was my son. I
remember thinking that. It was him. We were
standing on him, for Christ's sake. Then, I tasted
the wound, and it tasted like ash.

CAROLINE

Hold on.

PATTI

Bob's ash.

CAROLINE

Who's Bob?

PATTI

Fourteen years ago . . . I was cruising down a
country road when I spotted a bonfire. I slowed
the Harley down and noticed some people hov-
ering around its perimeter, chanting. I climbed
down the ravine and started out towards the fire.
I didn't want to startle them so I waved my
hands. I could smell something weird. One of
them came towards me and asked if he could
help. I wanted to ask what was burning but was
afraid I'd be next. It was smouldering, Caroline!
A curlicue of black smoke was rising and I
couldn't pry two syllables from my mouth! They
were cremating someone.

CAROLINE

A human?

PATTI

Would I like to join them, he asked.

CAROLINE

They were burning a person?

PATTI

And out of the trees they started to come.

CAROLINE

Jesus.

PATTI

They were all around me.

CAROLINE

My God! They didn't . . . ?

PATTI

No, no. They were nice . . . very normal . . .
not threatening. They offered me a glass of
champagne. They invited me to stay as they cir-
cled around the body . . . burning before us.
We burned him to a crisp. Then burned him
again until his bones became ash. One of them
brought out a shovel and scooped him up. I'll
never forget the sight of the warm ash . . . each
little pile giving off its own steam . . . and then
everyone took out containers . . . some put
him in a glass or a jar . . . Others put him in a
napkin or handkerchief. And somebody put
him in a large tin filled with bread dough and
baked him. And ate him. Just like my dream.

Shit. The guy I first met, the organizer, offered a piece to me. I took it. (*pause*) I liked that guy. I put him on the back of my bike and we spent a hundred miles together and one long imaginative evening in a clearing like this one. It was scary and fabulous and unlike anything I have felt before or since. The transformation of the body to ash, to bread, to pigment . . .

CAROLINE

You ate him?

PATTI

Yes.

CAROLINE

I can't believe this.

PATTI

We all had a bit of him. I certainly preferred it to those wafers I dangled on my tongue for those Catholic boyfriends I tried to please. (*pause*) My son tasted like him, Caroline. Bob's ashes tasted like my son. And I ate him.

CAROLINE

In your dreams.

PATTI

What's the difference? (*bends down and puts ear to the ground*) Hello. (*pause*) Have you ever made love here? Here on Gulliver's warm tummy?

CAROLINE

I have.

PATTI

You're lying.

CAROLINE

With a boy named Harry. Right here on this
dirt, this glorious dirt. We were so determined
to have a child. Immediately afterwards, Harry
held my knees up and then cupped me with
one hand while picking the long grass with the
other . . . to stop me up! Yes! Can you believe
him? I loved it. It was so natural. He put his
hand back over me and said he was just trying
to warm the grass. Then out of the trees they
started to come.

PATTI

What?

CAROLINE

Not as friendly as your group I'm afraid.

PATTI

What are you saying?!

CAROLINE

They made Harry pull the grass out. One blade
at a time.

PATTI

Jesus Christ.

CAROLINE

For art, they said.

PATTI

Art? They were artists?

CAROLINE

Like you.

PATTI

I don't understand.

CAROLINE

They were filmmakers. If we didn't fuck each
other, they were going to fuck me. Take one;
we made love in secret, we thought, and loved
it. Take two; we fucked for them.

PATTI

(*to herself*) Fantastic!

CAROLINE

Frightened bodies is what they got. The camera
whined and whined. I was so grateful to be on
my knees staring at the ground, trying to figure
out what the hell it was made of. When they
were finished, Harry and I just clung to each
other, then we moved into the trees, smeared in
a layer of dirt. I love this dirt.

PATTI

Smeared in a layer.

CAROLINE

This place kick-started my career.

PATTI

Pardon me?

CAROLINE

It's true. Right on this mound of granite and
moss.

PATTI

With a rape.

CAROLINE

And a love, goddammit. I found my life in a hiding place. And it's been very good to me. Who would have known I would be living above the treeline searching for fires?

PATTI

(*toasting*) To hiding places.

CAROLINE

From art.

PATTI

From art?

CAROLINE

That rapes.

PATTI

That's awful!

CAROLINE

No kidding. I can't look at the movie screen and not wonder what we looked like.

PATTI

Artists as criminals. As rapists. I can't believe it.

CAROLINE

You think art automatically equals morality?

PATTI

Of course not, but . . .

CAROLINE

Some of the best environmentalists I know are criminals.

PATTI

And sometimes the criminal in the artist can be advantageous.

CAROLINE

What happened to me is not art.

PATTI

Who knows what you became?

CAROLINE

Victim art. It's pathetic.

PATTI

Sometimes it works. You know Gauguin?

CAROLINE

Only that he fucked young Tahitian girls.

PATTI

There's a magnificent painting of a Tahitian girl lying face down on his yellow bed. Looking back in fear. What do you think she's afraid of?

CAROLINE

Looking back in fear? The person standing behind her?

PATTI

Exactly.

CAROLINE

The painter?

PATTI

What you have is the rapist painting the victim.

CAROLINE

Gauguin raped her? How do you know that?

PATTI

It's in her face.

CAROLINE

It's a painting, for Christ's sake!

PATTI

Like the face of cattle twisting back one last time.

CAROLINE

She was sacrificed.

PATTI

And inspired a masterpiece. And the end of a culture. But he saved her from disappearing.

CAROLINE

Give me a break.

PATTI

She doesn't know how lucky she is. He saved her memory.

CAROLINE

He saved his own.

PATTI

It's called "Spirit of the Dead Watching."

CAROLINE

He knew what he was painting about. Their
history is over.

PATTI

Except for the portraits to remind us who they
were.

CAROLINE

Without him, maybe the culture would still be
alive. What are you laughing at?

PATTI

The artist as conqueror. It's absurd.

CAROLINE

You love it. Look at you, your mouth is water-
ing.

PATTI

I remember getting goose bumps watching a
parade of design students march across a street,
all carrying large black portfolios at their sides.
The motion seemed threatening. It was fantastic. It must have felt as though you were carrying around a huge automatic weapon. I too
wanted to be armed. I too wanted to be a visual gangster. Knocking over the status quo.
Forcing a revolution off the canvas. Painting
the victims of the *coup d'état*.

CAROLINE

Face down on your bed.

PATTI

Let's take 'em from behind.

CAROLINE

The sheets smell of garlic and hibiscus.

PATTI

The bed must be yellow, like fire.

CAROLINE

You ain't sacrificing me.

PATTI

Not before your portrait. Otherwise what do
we have to remember you by?

CAROLINE

This! (CAROLINE *forces* PATTI's *arm behind her
back*)

PATTI

AH!

CAROLINE

Come on. Work for your art.

PATTI

Come to my studio. (CAROLINE *growls, then goes
for her bow and arrow*) What are you doing?

CAROLINE

I'm starving. Care for dinner?

PATTI

You're going to kill it?

CAROLINE

You'd be surprised what's left out there.
(*exiting*)

PATTI

Caroline?

CAROLINE

Build a fire. I won't be long. (*exits*)

PATTI *examines the knoll. Then starts to dig down into the knoll.
Notices something. Pulls out a tattered piece of linen. Notices bones
in hole. Grabs camera and photographs them repeatedly as we segue
to Scene Six where the* PRINCESS *secretly enters a wooded area.*

END OF SCENE FIVE.

SCENE SIX

A wooded area. The PRINCESS *runs on. Out of breath. Quickly hides while trying to stifle a giggle. She waits, then tiptoes around and spots one of her guardians she's escaping from. She kneels down and waits. Looks carefully around. Notices she has succeeded and quickly moves on only to realize she is alone.*

EGYPTIAN PRINCESS

(*slowly turns 360 degrees, whispering*) There's no one in my view. There's no one in my view! (*laughing*) No shadows to keep my distance from. I've done it. I'm brilliant. (*inhaling*) The air is full of cedar. I smell scribes and boats. (*hears something, frightened, quickly looks around*) I'm here! Game's over. I give up. (*no response. Notices a large hole*) Anyone down there? (*nervous giggle*) Hello in there! (*no response*) I'm coming down. Ready or not. Oh, the first step is warm. And the next has a dip like the palm of your hand. I feel wood under my toes. Now it's cool. And wet. Wet and . . . (*suddenly disappearing/off*) AHHH!

The echo of the "ahhh" will trail into CAROLINE *slowly turning around, posing for* PATTI *who is shooting her with a camera as we segue to Scene Seven in* PATTI'*s studio.*

END OF SCENE SIX.

SCENE SEVEN

PATTI's *studio. Live/work space.* PATTI *is shooting* CAROLINE *with a camera.* CAROLINE *is naked. The room is dark except for a spot on* CAROLINE. *There is a projector with a carousel of images already set up.* CAROLINE *is slowly turning.*

PATTI

(*as she shoots*) No. No . . . keep going.

CAROLINE

I'm not used to this.

PATTI

You're magnificent.

CAROLINE

Really?

PATTI

You're like a goddess.

CAROLINE

You're full of shit.

PATTI

My Diana. Hold it. Hold it. Keep looking back.

CAROLINE

(PATTI *starts the projector. images appear on* CARO-LINE's *body*) What are you doing? What's on me?

PATTI

All sorts of things.

CAROLINE

What is this?

PATTI

Just relax.

CAROLINE

⌐ Stones?

PATTI

Texture.

CAROLINE

Water.

PATTI

Volume.

CAROLINE

Clouds.

PATTI

Air.

CAROLINE

Bones.

PATTI

History.

CAROLINE

⌐ Willow.
└

PATTI

Hold it.

CAROLINE

I love willow.

PATTI

I love the grid on your body.

CAROLINE

(*wraps her arms around herself*) I feel as if I'm
being held.

PATTI

Hold tight!

CAROLINE

Tight as I can!

PATTI

Is this perfect or what? Keep talking.

CAROLINE

About what?

PATTI

Living above the tree line. You said you loved
it. Above the canopy.

CAROLINE

Because there's nothing but the sky above you
. . . no matter what the weather. You're alone
for 360 degrees, staring at an endless ceiling.
God, I remember spotting my first fire from
up there. I watched it break towards me like a

tidal wave and as I called out the longitude and latitude on the radio phone I realized the fire had a mind of its own. It was relentless. And natural. There's no fucking with nature, you know. Even now it's showing signs of revenge. They discovered a slow burning toxin in the soil. It can kill you in a second or it can take years. (*indicating* PATTI's *stomach*) May I feel him?

PATTI

(CAROLINE *moves her palm around* PATTI's *stomach searching for the baby*) Have any?

CAROLINE

One.

PATTI

Oh?

CAROLINE

A daughter.

PATTI

Really?

CAROLINE

Harry's and mine. There he is. Hello in there.

PATTI

Where is she?

CAROLINE

Buried in my knoll.

PATTI

(*realizing what she's dug up*) Oh.

CAROLINE

Yeah, under the willows. Where she was conceived and died. She hanged herself on her umbilical cord. And now I can't have any. It's weird to feel that no one is gaining on you. No fleshy legacy to rely on. Quick. Take a photo of the dodo who did it to herself. If that's not a perfect picture, then what is? Talk about sleeping through a drowning, I changed the plumbing without knowing what I was doing. And now I'm headed for extinction.

PATTI

Extinction?

CAROLINE

I'm so happy for you.

PATTI

(*to herself*) Bones and willow.

CAROLINE

I'd kill for a family.

PATTI

Mother and child.

CAROLINE

I know how hard it can be to raise a kid. If you ever need any help, you've got to let me know.

PATTI

Held together.

CAROLINE

You have no idea how much it would mean to
me. We could try.

PATTI

Like a suit of armour.

CAROLINE

If I get on your nerves, no hard feelings. We've
got plenty of time to figure it out before he
arrives. I just want to leave some kind of mark.
I'm the end of the line.

PATTI

Maybe not.

CAROLINE

What?

PATTI

I can help you.

CAROLINE

You can?

PATTI

I got it. I can save you.

CAROLINE

How?

PATTI

Let me use you. Let me use your daughter.
Please. Don't be afraid.

CAROLINE

Let me use your son. (*Pause.* PATTI *nods, then continues shooting feverishly as we segue to Scene Eight where the* EGYPTIAN PRINCESS *is being embalmed.*)

END OF SCENE SEVEN.

SCENE EIGHT

The PRINCESS *is standing or lying down with her wrists crossed over her heart. She is confident and hopeful. The sound is of jewels tumbling in water.*

EGYPTIAN PRINCESS

I'm taking my cat
and a snake
for a stick
and eleven bracelets
to reflect the light
of Osiris. Osiris.
I'm going to a brighter place.

They're making a slit along my side
fingers are searching
organs glide by.
How beautiful they are.
Like jewels
as they wash them
with palm wine and balsam.

They've taken the soft tissue out to dry
before they wrap it around an amulet
and place it back inside
my jar.
My heart is all
that remains
inside me.

I feel a thick black soaking
through my skin.
I'm being prepared.
I'm full of myrrh
and cinnamon.

I'm taking my cat
and a snake for a stick
and eleven bracelets.

Eleven bracelets.
I'm going to a brighter place.

END OF SCENE EIGHT.

As we segue to CAROLINE*'s bedroom where* STANLEY *and*
CAROLINE *are curled up in each other's arms.*

SCENE NINE

CAROLINE's *bedroom.* STANLEY *is lying in* CAROLINE's *arms. Her back is to us.* STANLEY *is looking downstage, over her shoulder. Morning light just in.*

STANLEY

You fell asleep.

CAROLINE

Ssshhh. Mmmmm. I dreamt I had a boy.

STANLEY

Fabulous evening.

CAROLINE

Oh, I bet you've said that to every member of your congregation.

STANLEY

No, no. I mean it.

CAROLINE

I know. I'm sorry. You're sweet . . . and brave. And delicious.

STANLEY

You were starving.

CAROLINE

I couldn't help it. I'm on a roll! (*bites him*)

STANLEY

Ow!

CAROLINE

I just love those cheeks, Stanley.

STANLEY

I love these. (*squeezing her ass. growls.*)

CAROLINE

Again. (*he does so*) Ow! (*growls*) You won't
believe this but you're my second ex-Rabbi.

STANLEY

What, are you on a quest?

CAROLINE

It's true. The other one is a hairdresser now. He
does very well. You'd love each other. You've got a
similar technique. And you both growl. I like that
too. I do. Maybe you know him. Rabbi Segal.

STANLEY

Sorry.

CAROLINE

No? He's just Kenneth now. Still looks after his
flock, though.

STANLEY

Really?

CAROLINE

He's got a synagogue full.

STANLEY

Lucky guy. They stuck by him and he still gets
to whisper into their ear.

CAROLINE

Some still need it.

STANLEY

Who doesn't? We're always looking for a little
reassurance. A few sweet nothings to soften the
blow of what lies ahead. (*short pause*)
Congregation. (*short pause*) I miss them.

CAROLINE

Now you're mine. (*starts to tickle him*)

STANLEY

No, no.

CAROLINE

Hold still.

STANLEY

Caroline!

CAROLINE

Blood to the surface! Blood to the surface!

STANLEY

God. You're wonderful. (*kiss*)

CAROLINE

You too.

STANLEY

Where have you come from? (*kiss*)

CAROLINE

The top of the forest. Tell me something. How does an ex-Rabbi make a living?

STANLEY

Life insurance.

CAROLINE

You sell life insurance?

STANLEY

I'm realistic.

CAROLINE

I should say so. What happened to your congregation?

STANLEY

Oh, I've been excommunicated. I should warn you I'm more ritual than I am God. It's true. You see, I hate the pulpit. I prefer being down on the floor with them, sitting at their kitchen tables debating beneficiaries and faith. That policy. That trust. Gotta have it.

CAROLINE

That trust.

STANLEY

Otherwise I can't pay the rent. And I make the odd cut.

CAROLINE

Cut? You're a moyle?

46

STANLEY

I'm very good.

CAROLINE

Oh my God!

STANLEY

I take refuge in the ritual.

CAROLINE

(*to herself*) Like slitting throats. I'm sorry.

STANLEY

No, no. You're right. (*smiles. pause.*) Look, I hope
you don't think I'm a whacko, but sometimes
when I hold up that baby penis by the throat,
its little hole seems like a frightened mouth to
me. And then I attach the clamp and the mouth
cries open. Slitting throats is not too far off,
Caroline. But there's a collective grinding of the
teeth when I make my cut. There's a history to
that groan. That's what the ritual provides. A
rationale for cutting. God bless rituals. They
cushion the anxiety of watching yourself invol-
untarily swing too far out, which on occasion
can be a good thing.

CAROLINE

Were you a bad boy, Stanley?

STANLEY

I became a Rabbi, didn't I?

CAROLINE

Married?

STANLEY

Once to a Barbara O'Connor. Blonde. Green
eyes. She got tired of watching me think and
ran off and married a nine-to-five dud. I ran
off to the Yeshiva dreaming of Thomas Merton
and contemplation. I was looking for the Judaic
equivalent of a Trappist monk. I should have
converted to Catholicism. I needed the scholar-
ship, the monastic life. The devotion, the robes,
the sandals. It would have anaesthetized my
demons.

CAROLINE

Children?

STANLEY

Me? Nope. Never.

CAROLINE

Gonna die alone?

STANLEY

Who doesn't?

CAROLINE

Right.

STANLEY

I want to be cremated. Like my father. In the
great outdoors.

CAROLINE

You burned him?

STANLEY

Then made him into bread. And broke it.

CAROLINE

And ate him?

STANLEY

What's in ash, anyway? We were starving. We
needed him. We kneaded the hell out of him.
Then we washed him down with champagne.

CAROLINE

Jesus. How long ago?

STANLEY

Fourteen. Fifteen years. I don't know. Why?

CAROLINE

Bob . . .

STANLEY

Shit.

CAROLINE

Oh my God. I can't believe this.

STANLEY

You can't? How did you know him?

CAROLINE

Do you remember taking a ride on a Harley
after the cremation? A young girl on a motor-
cycle.

STANLEY

Yes. Yes. Of course I do! After the ceremony . . .
Patti . . . Christ. How the hell would you know
her?

CAROLINE

I saved her life.

STANLEY

How?

CAROLINE

From drowning.

STANLEY

Poor baby.

CAROLINE

She swam out too far.

STANLEY

She was the bravest girl I ever met. It was an amazing night. She told me that she was on her way to a different state of mind. And she thought she could drive there. Drive there! Who the hell drives there these days?

CAROLINE

She's four months' pregnant. And I'm gonna help raise that kid.

STANLEY

That's very generous of you. Who's the father?

CAROLINE

I think he's Asian.

STANLEY

Wonderful. Bringing ancient cultures together to survive the onslaught. I like it. I hope the baby learns Chinese.

CAROLINE

The onslaught?

STANLEY

Can't you feel the change in the social tempera-
ture? It's giddy with fear out there. The spiritual
biz is booming and for good reason. This whole
Judeo-Christian madness is on the way out,
everyone knows it. And it's terrifying. They've
removed the door handles! So, an Asian Jew? A
little mix and match might be a good thing to
help ward off the last rampage. Here it comes!
Better find yourself a refuge.

CAROLINE

I have.

STANLEY

Good thinking. I haven't. Yet.

CAROLINE

How did he die?

STANLEY

What?

CAROLINE

How did your father die?

STANLEY

Oh, I killed him.

CAROLINE

What do you mean you killed him?

STANLEY

He had Alzheimer's. I watched him slowly
become an idiot . . . shouting at mirrors. We
had to cover them and then he became a baby.
He was uncontrollable. The sisterhood made
large diapers for him.

CAROLINE

So you killed him?

STANLEY

It's what he wanted. At a certain point.

CAROLINE

Smart.

STANLEY

He was in my hands . . . and then he wasn't. I
don't know . . . the spirit has weight and Dad
lost it. I held his house. I held his house. It was
a good thing to do. Unfortunately, I lost my job
over it. I think it had more to do with the cremation than the killing. It disgusted my flock.

CAROLINE

Would you ever kill again?

STANLEY

Only for the money. No, no. Absolutely not.

CAROLINE

For good reason?

STANLEY

There is no good reason. Believe me. Oh. I'm
sorry. Have you got someone . . . ?

CAROLINE

No, no.

STANLEY

A parent? That could be tough.

CAROLINE

No, no.

STANLEY

A friend?

CAROLINE

No. (*pause*) Me.

STANLEY

You? You're dying?

CAROLINE

I am.

STANLEY

Of what?

CAROLINE

What's the difference? I just don't want to die
on a ventilator. Help me.

STANLEY

You want me to kill you? I just met you! Tell
me you have a morbid sense of humour,
Caroline.

CAROLINE

I'm only being realistic. Will you think about it?

STANLEY

I can't think about it.

CAROLINE

No one has to know.

STANLEY

We do.

CAROLINE

Please.

STANLEY

You're having a kid, for Christ's sake!

CAROLINE

We're having a boy.

STANLEY

Then celebrate it. Look, why don't we discuss this some other time, say thirty years in the future?

CAROLINE

I have a name for him, Stanley.

STANLEY

I'd like to hear it. (*pause*)

END OF SCENE NINE.

We notice PATTI *feverishly cutting willow, very excited, as we segue to Scene Ten.*

54

SCENE TEN

The PRINCESS *is manipulating an undetermined length of linen. She is still and serene as if she's lying in her sarcophagus. She is humming to herself. It is a warm, contented sound. She is moving the linen around as if her arms are independent of her body. She stretches the material, wrapping it around her shoulders like a shawl and then covering different parts of her body. She stops and listens. We hear the distant crumbling of a wall. She puts the linen down. Now the sound of a wall being pushed through.*

EGYPTIAN PRINCESS

What's that? Who's there? Oh, am I there already? But I haven't heard the river yet. Or have I? Am I really here? (*staring into the face of her kidnappers*) AH! Who are you? Servants of Osiris . . . eight hands lifting me up to the light . . . sailing through to another world! Thank you. Thank you! Finally. I'm ready.

We should have a sense of an empty space as we segue to Scene Eleven, where we hear an excited knocking at PATTI's *door by* CAROLINE. *The* PRINCESS *is humming the opening bars to "I'm taking my cat" as a light source reveals an abrupt opening of the door.*

END OF SCENE TEN.

 **SCENE ELEVEN**

Door to PATTI*'s studio.* CAROLINE *and* STANLEY *are waiting.*
CAROLINE *is knocking.* PRINCESS *speaks offstage during the following scene.*

EGYPTIAN PRINCESS

I'm taking my cat
and a snake
for a stick
and eleven bracelets.
Eleven bracelets.
I'm going to a brighter place.

PATTI *opens door.*

CAROLINE

We're here!

PATTI

You're early. And, by the way, I need some
more willow. Can I get it? What? Who's that?

CAROLINE

Dinner.

STANLEY

Hi Patti.

PATTI

No. Oh my God! Stanley?

EGYPTIAN PRINCESS

I'm taking my cat
and a snake for a stick

and eleven bracelets.
Eleven bracelets.
I'm going to a brighter place.

END OF SCENE ELEVEN.
END OF ACT ONE.

Act Two

SCENE TWELVE

A WEEK LATER

The knoll. Day. Beautiful light. STANLEY *is posing nude for* CARO-
LINE. *She's drawing him.* PATTI *enters dragging a bale of willows.*

STANLEY

I'd think twice about that.

PATTI

I said, no. And why are we . . .

STANLEY

The longer you wait the more painful it is.

PATTI

The baby's not due for five months.

CAROLINE

Keep still.

PATTI

By the way, Stanley, circumcision is nothing
more than a hygienic solution elevated to
Jewish law and underwritten by the hand of
God. Like kosher.

STANLEY

It was a covenant with God, Patti. If you want
to think of it as a health issue then do. It
should get done.

PATTI

Look, teaching little boys to properly clean themselves seems more appropriate than whacking off their foreskin. And no, I don't find the uninitiated unattractive. I've had both, thank you. And besides, what does it matter when it's wrapped in latex? It's all we feel now, that latex. And sooner or later it too will be integrated into the ritual to such a degree that it will become law and eventually God will co-sign the latex bill. The word will come forth! A rule will be born. You watch. It's no different than the elevation of your cut from hygienic to spiritual. God's cock rule.

CAROLINE

Whoa!

PATTI

The one we made up for Him. (*tightens the knot of the bale and winces like the* EGYPTIAN PRINCESS *in Scene Two.*)

STANLEY

You believe that?

PATTI

Don't we make it all up? Even Him and His duties?

STANLEY

It's an historical link. You can't deny history. It binds us together.

PATTI

I'm not denying history. It's an old fear solidi-fied into ritual. And it's the fear that binds us

60

together. Not the history. We've got to put a
stop to it. Kill the ritual, kill the fear.

STANLEY

You don't understand, this is more than break-
ing a ritual. It's five thousand years old, for
Christ's sake.

PATTI

So?

STANLEY

You're not a man. He'll look beautiful.
Proportioned. Clean. Popular. He'll kill you for
not doing it.

PATTI

Matricide for cosmetics? Is that what I have to
look forward to? It's barbaric.

STANLEY

Are we taking a break?

CAROLINE

(*continuing drawing*) Not yet.

PATTI

(*comes over to* CAROLINE. *stands behind her and
observes her drawing. looks at* STANLEY, *then at the
drawing*) You've given him horns.

STANLEY

You have?

CAROLINE

Be still.

PATTI

And she's been very kind as well. If I may say
so myself.

CAROLINE

I love minotaurs. When did they go extinct?

PATTI

With Picasso. He killed them off like the buffalo.

STANLEY

May I see it?

CAROLINE

I'm afraid not.

STANLEY

Why?

CAROLINE

It's not ready to be seen.

STANLEY

But Patti has.

CAROLINE

She likes it.

STANLEY

Well, how do you know whether . . . ?

CAROLINE

I can't take the chance. You'll just have to live
with it. (*kisses him*)

STANLEY

Thanks.

PATTI

You've got a beautiful body for drawing,
Stanley.

STANLEY

Why thank you.

PATTI

Where'd you get it?

STANLEY

From my Dad.

PATTI

Me too. Except I'm bigger. Turn around.

STANLEY

Her father was a jockey.

PATTI

I am the daughter of Joshua. Winner of a thousand rides. (*brief pause*) Get down, Rabbi!

STANLEY

What?

PATTI

On all fours. Just once around the track. How's
your back?

CAROLINE

Strong.

PATTI

I'll show you what Dad was known for. Get down.

STANLEY

You're going to get on my back?

PATTI

Yes. Here. (*giving* CAROLINE *a camera*) There may be a photo finish.

CAROLINE

What about the baby?

PATTI

The baby's fine.

STANLEY

You rode your father?

PATTI

Every chance I got. (STANLEY *gets down on his knees, leans forward on his elbows as* PATTI *gets up on him.*) I remember clearing the living room. Dad chomping at the bit. My leg swinging over his back. The clang of the bell and we were off! (*she tries lying on top of his body with her mouth in his ear, whispering*) "Come on, beauty. Let's go!" (*kicking him in the ribs*)

STANLEY

OW!

PATTI

Faster. Dad believed in riding "as one body." Over every bump and mud patch. Constantly whispering into the horse's ear, "Come on, beauty."

STANLEY

Wait a minute.

PATTI

"Let's go!" (*kicking him again*)

STANLEY

OW!

PATTI

FASTER!

STANLEY

I'm trying.

PATTI

Not good enough!

STANLEY

Shit!

PATTI

FASTER ! FASTER! Circling the room, hanging on to his collar as we crashed through the thread I set up between two chairs.

CAROLINE

Winner by a nose!

CAROLINE, PATTI AND STANLEY

(*celebrating*) YES!

CAROLINE

Stanley? Are you all right?

STANLEY

I'm fabulous.

PATTI

I grew up riding my father. (*dismounting*)

STANLEY

He taught you well.

PATTI

And then he left, the bastard. So, I graduated to
Harleys. You smelled like my father for a moment
there, Stanley.

STANLEY

I suspected it.

CAROLINE

Is that why you kicked him?

PATTI

I just knew we could win. And so did he, didn't
you? (PATTI *kisses* STANLEY *with authority*)

STANLEY

Well . . .

CAROLINE

Hey! What are you doing?

PATTI

What jockey doesn't kiss her mount? Thank

you, Stanley. It's exactly what I needed.

STANLEY

My pleasure.

CAROLINE

What about the owner?

PATTI

I love you. (PATTI *kisses* CAROLINE *with the same authority*) It's funny kissing a one-night stand fourteen years later. Do you remember that night, Stanley?

STANLEY

Maybe.

PATTI

We sprinkled Bob over our fingers.

STANLEY

Uh huh.

PATTI

And drew him all over our bodies.

CAROLINE

You did what?

PATTI

We decorated ourselves. I drew an arrow on his cock. He drew one through my nipples.

CAROLINE

What the hell were you doing?

67

PATTI

Playing Cupid with Bob's ashes. I'll never forget the taste. I remember tasting Bob on your
lips. You know, Stanley, you took up a year's
worth of my dreams. We crossed a line together
and it worked. I felt I could do anything after
that night. Maybe we need to go far, far out
there to rejuvenate ourselves back into exis-
tence. Crossing a border might help.

CAROLINE

You fucked with your father's ashes?

PATTI

Your father?

CAROLINE

Why didn't you tell me?

PATTI

I ate your father?

CAROLINE

You must have known this would come up.

PATTI

You fucked me with your father's ashes?

STANLEY

It was fourteen years ago.

PATTI

That's incredible.

CAROLINE

You fucked with the dead.

PATTI

Literally.

STANLEY

He made me kill him.

PATTI

I'm going out of my mind.

CAROLINE

"Made"?

PATTI

You killed your father?

STANLEY

He wanted me to . . . he wanted me to before
the Alzheimer's did. I tried giving him an
overdose but he threw it up. I had no choice. I
had to complete it. I couldn't live with him
surviving. He wanted me to do it. I pressed
that pillow into his face with all my might . . .
until I was left alone. And suddenly I loved
him as if his death opened a door, but now he
wasn't there. He wasn't there. I missed him. I
mean, I loved him, finally. I was never good
enough until I killed him. I did a good job
though. And then he disappeared. I celebrated
his end that day. It was glorious. I felt I was
finally through with him. His body . . . up in
smoke, signalling the horizon that he was finished. Thank God for rituals.

PATTI

He's not finished, Stanley.

STANLEY

What do you mean?

PATTI

I saved him. *(holding out film container of ash)* I always wanted to do this, to give him back to you.

STANLEY

You kept it?

PATTI

I keep everything. (STANLEY *opens container*) He tasted like my son, Stanley.

CAROLINE

In your dreams.

PATTI

What's the difference? *(pause)* You've come for your dad, haven't you? We're all together now. It's perfect.

STANLEY

Not yet. (STANLEY *takes the ash from* PATTI *and tosses it back into his mouth*)

PATTI AND CAROLINE

Oh my God! (PATTI *is excited,* CAROLINE's *horrified*)

CAROLINE

Stanley, don't!

PATTI

Fantastic.

STANLEY

(*chews the ash and tries swallowing it, mumbling, he chews and drinks*) Ahhh, nothing like a good symbolic ingestion to crank up a new horizon. Clear the frame and start over.

CAROLINE

This is crazy.

PATTI

No, it's brave.

CAROLINE

You can't do this.

STANLEY

There's nothing to this shit.

CAROLINE

There's a lot to that shit.

STANLEY

Not any more.

CAROLINE

How can you say that? You finished him off. There's nothing left.

STANLEY

There's nothing to worry about.

CAROLINE

I don't want to be burned and eaten and fucked with, Stanley!

PATTI

What are you talking about?

CAROLINE

Respect!

STANLEY

Taking care of each other in our old age. Our future, Patti.

CAROLINE

Yeah, I need all the future I can get.

PATTI

I'm doing something about that.

CAROLINE

You are?

PATTI

(*kisses* CAROLINE *on cheek*) Come. See for yourself.

LIGHTS OUT.
END OF SCENE TWELVE.

SCENE THIRTEEN

Opens with the sound of aquatic transport. A barge full of mummies. We then hear the collective sound of fearful voices, rising to a pitch.

EGYPTIAN PRINCESS

There are others here!
I'm not alone.
We're going together.
I hear the oars
and the gigantic sail.
The water is high.
There's been a flood.
We're on our way.
We're going together.
I'm not alone.
I feel the rudder
and, OH! OH!
I'm rising now
toward a light.
I can smell it.
We're getting closer.
It's too bright.
We're almost there.
I can't see.
Its embrace
is burning me.

(pause)

We hear the metallic scoop of a large shovel several times as we segue to PATTI's studio.

END OF SCENE THIRTEEN.

SCENE FOURTEEN

PATTI's *live/work space. Hanging in mid-air is a sculptural form using materials of* CAROLINE's *history. For example, woven willow, woven film, by itself and with willow and bone. Photographs of* CAROLINE *slashed with thick black brushstrokes. Moss from the knoll.*

CAROLINE

That's me?

PATTI

That's part of you.

CAROLINE

What part?

STANLEY

From your right mole to your left hip. Am I right?

CAROLINE

I think so.

PATTI

You're still in progress. I mean, it's very rough right now.

CAROLINE

You've woven me through the willow.

PATTI

I'm just assembling . . .

CAROLINE

No, no. I like it.

74

STANLEY

It looks like a corset. A ribcage.

PATTI

Think armour. I'd like to put it on you.

CAROLINE

And photograph it?

PATTI

Yes.

STANLEY

Your self as armour.

CAROLINE

I need all the protection I can get. (*kisses* STAN-
LEY)

PATTI

You'll get it.

CAROLINE

That black line? What's that? It's not ash, is it?

PATTI

No, no. Well, it was.

CAROLINE

Human?

PATTI

Yes . . .

CAROLINE

What?

PATTI

(*notices* STANLEY *handling a precious urn*) CARE-
FUL! Don't spill it! There's half an ounce of
Egyptian essence in there. I always keep it
nearby. It inspires me. It's the perfect transformation of a life I know of. Bodies to science
are a dime a dozen. This is unique. It's a shellac.
A veneer made from the bodies of Egyptian
mummies. They call it True Mummy.

CAROLINE

Human veneer?

STANLEY

You're lying!

CAROLINE

On me?

PATTI

Just a smear. I rub it on everything I make. I
keep the Egyptians alive that way. It's fantastic!
When the Egyptians prepared their dead, they
filled the bodies with asphaltum. So the cavity
would maintain its shape. The pyramids were
never intended as their final resting place. They
were on a journey. They were dreaming themselves to Osiris. But the pyramids were robbed.
The mummies were stolen and shipped to
Europe. When the robbers were discovered, they
burned the evidence … thousands of mummies. And then a chemist discovered that the
ashes from the burnt mummies produced the
best shellac in the history of art. True Mummy.

76

A deep, gorgeous, mature, clear glaze that artists spread across their canvasses for two hundred years. Preserving their work with the bodies of Egyptians. Turner, for one! His watery land-scapes are literally sealed in flesh and bone.

STANLEY

Recycled mummies!

CAROLINE

My God!

PATTI

That's the glue! (*laughing*) Sort of dispels the myth about what holds a work of art together. (*laughing*)

CAROLINE

Humans sacrificed for art.

PATTI

Humans protecting their dreams. Their future. Their legacy.

CAROLINE

With the bodies of others.

STANLEY

With a sacred veneer.

PATTI

Isn't that gorgeous?

STANLEY

What symmetry!

CAROLINE

You like this?

STANLEY

I wouldn't mind knowing that my body was being used to protect a Turner. Turner, Caroline. You know what that means? Living out your immortal self in the Tate Gallery. Never alone, feeling the proximity of warm bodies as they lean in to examine a thick brush stroke. "I'm over here!"

PATTI

I've decided to mix the willow with bones. The ingredient that made the willow so strong. You see, if I weave them together with linen …

CAROLINE

Whose bones?

PATTI

Your daughter's, I believe. I hope. See that?

CAROLINE

What?

PATTI

Not to worry. I've taken very good care of them.

CAROLINE

You dug them up?

PATTI

When you asked me to make a fire, remember?

78

STANLEY

You collect bodies?

CAROLINE

Those are my daughter's bones?

PATTI

Yes. Yes! Aren't they beautiful? I wanted you to
see it for yourself. I thought you'd love the
idea, the homecoming. The two of you becom-
ing the material of your own legacy. They're
like little twigs, aren't they?

CAROLINE

Jesus Christ!

PATTI

(CAROLINE *starts to pull the bones out of the form*)
Hey! Wait a second. What are you doing? Don't
touch that!

STANLEY

Caroline?

CAROLINE

This is my baby! You can't just dig her up and
USE HER. Who the hell do you think you are?
That ground is hers, Patti! She was conceived,
born, and died there. And we are meant to be
in it together. That dirt and bone and willow
are alive. Pieces of ourselves. Feel them. They
are not just material for your art. This is my
daughter.

PATTI

I'm trying to make a new life out of them,

Caroline. There's magic in this reunion. Believe
me, I know what I'm talking about. You'll live
forever.

CAROLINE

That's bullshit! It's sacrilege! It's not going to
transform us. It's a desecration.

PATTI

Exactly! That's why it has power. It's sacred.
Otherwise they're just dead symbols.

CAROLINE

They're real.

PATTI

In fact . . . I say let's go farther. Let's burn part
of the willow and bones and make a shellac.

CAROLINE

Wait a minute.

STANLEY

Her baby as veneer?

CAROLINE

You are not going to take the living growth
from the body of my daughter and use it as
kindling to make a shellac to protect . . .

PATTI

Your history. Your self. Your future. That willow,
and your daughter, may be covered by a mall in
a few years. And I want to take advantage of that
extinction by preserving the two of you. Now!

CAROLINE

Extinction? I thought this was going to be a living idea. I'm alive, I'm here.

PATTI

Thank God.

CAROLINE

Would you want me to fool with your son's bones? God forbid he dies in childbirth.

PATTI

If it was meant to remember him, then yes.

CAROLINE

Put her back. (*referring to bones*)

PATTI

No, no. Please, let me explain. Give me a chance, Caroline. I'm not going to harm her. This is beautiful what I'm doing. You'll see, it'll be perfect.

CAROLINE

I hate fire.

PATTI

I'm protecting your future.

CAROLINE

You're a cannibal.

PATTI

I'm a saviour. (CAROLINE *stumbles*)

CAROLINE

Shit!

PATTI

Give it to me.

STANLEY

Caroline?

CAROLINE

Damn.

STANLEY

Caroline!

PATTI

What's wrong?

STANLEY

(*to* PATTI) I don't know.

CAROLINE

Stanley.

STANLEY

Oh sweetheart.

PATTI

I'm pleading with you.

STANLEY

Please be quiet.

CAROLINE

No, no. It's time.

STANLEY

That's not true.

PATTI

What does she want?

CAROLINE

Put them back.

PATTI

Of course. Anything you say. But if I were you . . .

CAROLINE

You know . . . I've thought of a name for the
baby.

STANLEY

Everything's going to be all right.

CAROLINE

Karel with a K. (*laughs*) Do it, Stanley.

PATTI

Do what? What are you talking about? Don't
touch her! She's alive. NO! NO! She's not going
anywhere. We made a deal. My baby needs her.
Caroline! Fuck, Stanley, do something! What
about my baby? Don't you want him? *Caroline*!
Don't you want him? (PATTI *puts* CAROLINE*'s
hand on her belly*) Feel him. FEEL HIM.

Action mirrors lifesaving in Scene One. Long pause. Lights dim. PATTI *exits. Lights up on* STANLEY *at knoll draping* CAROLINE'*s body. He kneels down beside her. We hear the sound of the grinding pestle in mortar as we segue to Scene Fifteen.*

END OF SCENE FOURTEEN.

SCENE FIFTEEN

Open with the sound of the grinding of the pestle on the mortar. We also hear the occasional drip. The PRINCESS' *voice is weak and fading, which could be incorporated into a vocal gesture. Now an intense sound of resistance against the pestle is heard.*

EGYPTIAN PRINCESS

(*off*) There are still bones
and cartilage
and skin
and

(*intense sound of resistance against the pestle*)

There are still bones.

Lights down as we segue to the knoll where STANLEY *is kneeling next to the body of* CAROLINE. *A shovel rests on the ground.*

END OF SCENE FIFTEEN.

SCENE SIXTEEN

CAROLINE's *body is lying on the knoll. Draped.* STANLEY *is squatting beside her. Long pause.* PATTI *appears, dragging a bunch of willows.*

STANLEY

What are you doing? I'm gonna dig a hole. It's what she wanted. It's why we're here. Hold on, Patti!

PATTI

She needs to burn.

STANLEY

You're not going to burn her.

PATTI

Oh yes I am. I need her ash to complete her legacy. And you're going to help me.

STANLEY

She's going to get what she wanted.

PATTI

How do you know what she wanted?

STANLEY

She told me.

PATTI

She wanted legacy. And, boy, we'll give it to her.

STANLEY

What's gotten into you?

86

PATTI

She's dead and I have to take advantage of it.

STANLEY

Over my dead body.

PATTI

If that's what it takes, Stanley.

STANLEY

You're nuts.

PATTI

We both are, sweetheart.

STANLEY

You can't burn her.

PATTI

You burned your father and ate him. And who
says we shouldn't decorate ourselves again?

STANLEY

Jesus.

PATTI

We'll film it this time. Caroline all over our
bodies.

STANLEY

You're out of your mind.

PATTI

I haven't been clearer in years.

STANLEY

Then film the body. Yeah. Film the digging.
Film the throwing of the dirt on to her. Get a
close-up of her disappearing. Make this a truly
sacred space. Where she and the bones of her
daughter are finally laid to rest. Give them a
chance to be together. Honour them. Let your
son know of this place.

PATTI

You're heartwarming, Stan. You must be a man of
the cloth. Sentimental. Sorry, but I need to do this.
I have no choice. I need ash. Mummy. Veneer.

STANLEY

And that entitles you to fuck over someone
you loved so much? You loved her. You did!
(PATTI *starts to shoot the body with the camcorder*)

PATTI

She knew the whole time she was dying!

STANLEY

THERE WILL BE NO BURNING HERE.

PATTI

Get the fuck out of my way.

STANLEY

I'm not moving.

PATTI

I'm going to burn her. And turn her body into
a shellac. (*kicks the body*)

STANLEY

Goddamn you.

PATTI

(*maneuvers* STANLEY *away from body*) I loved you!

STANLEY

Don't you dare do that again!

PATTI

(*falls to knees and punches the body*) You fucking
bitch! (*hugs the body*) You were here. You were
here. (*crying. hugs herself. pause.*)

STANLEY

Look, we'll make a beautiful gravesite for her.
Where do you suggest? Over there? Beside the
willows? She'd love it here. I know how you
feel, Patti. I'm afraid, too. I love you, Patti. I do.
We could help each other. I'm very good at a
whole bunch of things. I'm a quick learner,
too. The baby will like me.

PATTI

(*feels her baby move*) Shit.

STANLEY

What?

PATTI

Nothing.

STANLEY

We need each other.

PATTI

No, Stanley, we needed her. And now I've got
fuck all.

STANLEY

Except your son. For God's sake, Patti, listen to
me! I need you. Caroline needs you. (PATTI *gives
him the camera*) What are you doing? Don't give
this to me! Wait a minute! Where are you
going? (*quickly gathering her things*) I don't
understand. You're giving up?

PATTI

I've got to get out of here!

STANLEY

And go where? To a different state of mind?
What are you going to do? Drive there? Drive
there! (*pause*) She's all I've got.

PATTI

Then take good care of her. (PATTI *starts to exit*)

STANLEY

(*puts the camcorder down. looks at the body. gets*
CAROLINE's *daughter's bones and puts them on her
body. gets his shovel. goes over to where he wants to
dig. digs. stops, then quietly says the opening lines of
the Mourner's Prayer, The Kaddash*) Yisqadal
v'yiskaddash sh'may rabboh . . . b'olmah dee-
v'roh chirusay v'yamlich malchusay. . . (*starts to
cry/starts to dig*)

LIGHTS DOWN.

END OF SCENE SIXTEEN. SEGUE TO A PAINTING BY TURNER.

SCENE SEVENTEEN

An extremely detailed image of a Turner painting is revealed. We should be able to see the texture and thickness of the brushstrokes. Long pause. Long enough for us to realize that the EGYPTIAN PRINCESS *is on it.*

Suggestion: Turner's painting, "The Slavers Throwing the Dead and Dying Overboard."

END

TOM CONE's plays have been produced throughout Canada, the United States, England, and Australia. He currently lives in Vancouver.